basketball

Consultants

George King, athletic
director
Purdue University
West Lafayette, Indiana

Dave Toney, assistant
basketball coach
Purdue University

Demonstrators

Ty Bedford
George Faerber
Bob Ford
Bill Franklin
Jerry Johnson
Frank Kaufman
Bill Kroc
Steve Longfellow
Brad McNulty
Rick Mount
Kenny Otto
Rick Risinger
Jim Rogers
Randy Thompson
Larry Weatherford

published by:

The Athletic Institute

Merchandise Mart, Chicago

*A not-for-profit organization
devoted to the advancement of
athletics, physical education
and recreation.*

Robert G. Bluth, *editor*

**Library of Congress
Catalog Card Number 79-109498**

**"Sports Techniques" Series
SBN·87670-036-9**

**Published by The Athletic Institute
Chicago, Illinois 60654**

Foreword

The **"Sports Techniques" Series** is a comprehensive set of instructional aids in sports which are made available by The Athletic Institute. This book is part of a master plan which seeks to make the benefits of athletics, physical education and recreation available to everyone.

The Athletic Institute, a not-for-profit organization devoted to the advancement of athletics, physical education and recreation, believes that sports participation by young and old has benefits of inestimable value to the individual.

The nature and scope of the many Institute programs are determined by nationally-known professional educators who are noted for their outstanding knowledge and expertise in their fields.

The Institute believes that through this book the reader will become more proficient and skilled in the fundamentals of this fine sport. Knowledge and the practice necessary to mold knowledge into playing ability are the keys to real enjoyment in playing any game or sport.

Donald E. Bushore
Executive Director
The Athletic Institute

Introduction

The game of basketball affords all players a challenging team sport opportunity. It offers participants a chance to experience extremes of physical and mental effort.

The diverse elements of the game call for finesse, power, accuracy, stamina, grace, quickness, strength and agility. Of course, attributes of determination, concentration, relaxation and organization are also important to successful play. Players must individualize skills in one-on-one confrontations and collective skills during team play.

Satisfaction from playing this game has motivated both men and women who possess varied levels of skill to enjoy basketball in our country and countries throughout the world.

Table of Contents

basic stances

Basic Offensive Stance

The *basic offensive stance,* sometimes referred to as the **ready position,** gives a player three avenues of attack: 1) to drive on a defender (dribble), 2) to shoot over defender, 3) to pass to a teammate.

This position affords proper body balance with feet a shoulder's-width apart and one foot slightly ahead of the other. Head is up, shoulders are square to the basket and knees are slightly flexed. Ball is held firmly from chest to waist level.

1. **BASIC OFFENSIVE STANCE**
   Feet Are Shoulder's-Width Apart.
   One Foot Slightly Ahead of the Other.
   Head Up.
   Shoulders and Body Square to Hoop.
   Ball Held Firmly at Chest Level.

2. **FROM BASIC OFFENSIVE STANCE, PLAYER MAY REACT QUICKLY FOR DRIVE TO BASKET, SHOT IF OPEN OR PASS TO TEAMMATE.**

Basic Defensive Stance

Like the offensive ready position, the *basic defensive stance* requires proper body position and weight distribution for quick movements and reactions according to the changing defensive situation.

A defender must be ready to counter the three basic options available to the offensive player—the drive, shot or pass. Good defense involves anticipation of the next movement by the offensive player and quick reactions to move and control these movements effectively.

As a defensive player, position yourself just beyond

1. **DEFENSIVE READY POSITION**
   **Body Balanced with Weight Equally
      Distributed on Both Feet.**
   **Feet Are Shoulder's-Width Apart with
      One Foot Slightly Ahead of the Other.**
   Knees Are Flexed.
   Arms Are Relatively Close to Body.
   Head Is Up with Eyes Focused Ahead.

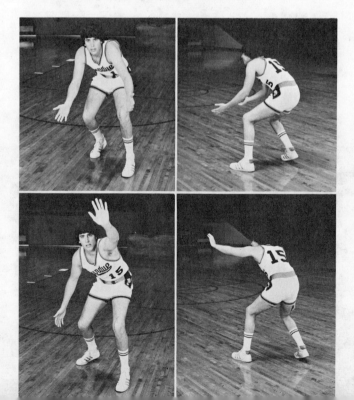

a normal arm's reach from the opponent with the ball, then make the necessary adjustments to the opponent's moves. From this point it is a matter of anticipating what the defender is going to do and reacting accordingly.

To overplay an opponent effectively, take one half-step to the side which you wish to defend. Proper defensive movement employs a sliding action of the feet. Take your first step in the direction in which the opponent starts his move. Your second step is a sliding step to bring you into a control position. This sequence is then repeated as required.

When guarding a man without the ball, adjust your position so you see both your opponent and the ball on the court. Any movement of the offensive player must be countered. Any movement of the ball most likely will require an adjustment on your part. Preventing "your man" from getting the ball at all is your best defense.

2. OVERPLAY OPPONENT ONE HALF-STEP TO THE SIDE YOU WISH TO DEFEND.

3. USE STEP, SLIDING-STEP ACTION TO ACHIEVE CONTROL POSITION.

4. CLOSE TO POSITION IN DRIBBLER'S PATH.

5. WHEN DEFENDING AGAINST SHOOTER, RAISE CLOSEST HAND AND MOVE TO TIGHTER POSITION. LIKEWISE, WHEN DEFENDING AGAINST PASS, REACT WITH HAND CLOSEST TO SOURCE OF PASS.

dribble

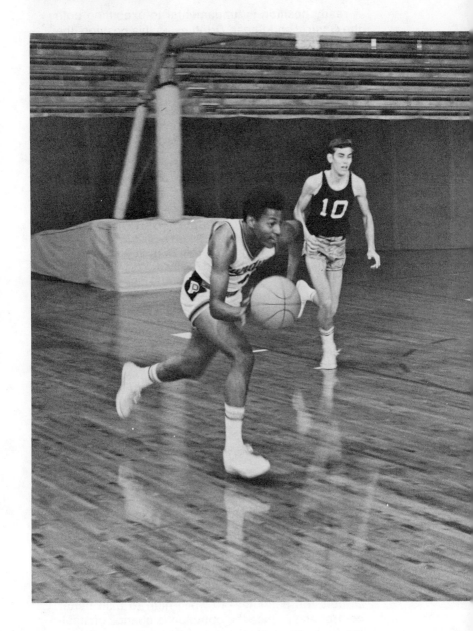

Basic Dribble Position

A **ready position** is fundamental to executing both the *Control* and *Speed Dribbles.* In this position, the head is up, knees are flexed, eyes focus down floor, and the body is in a semi-crouched position. The degree of body crouch varies according to the speed of the dribble and the conditions under which the dribbler performs.

The finger and thumb tips contact the ball. The hand is on top of the ball toward the back half of the top surface.

BASIC DRIBBLE POSITION
Head Up; Eyes Focus Ahead.
Knees Flexed; Body in Semi-Crouched Position.
Ball Contacted with Finger and Thumb Tips.
Free Arm is Out for Balance and Ball Protection.

Control Dribble

Begin by projecting the ball slightly forward using fingertip control. Fingertip control is executed by flexing of the wrist and fingers. The lower arm from the elbow to fingertips moves in a pumping action to project, receive and then project the ball again.

Dribble the ball knee- to waist-high to gain better control and reduce the opponent's chance of stealing it. Again, protect the ball with the arm and leg nearest your opponent.

1. ASSUME READY POSITION.
2. PROJECT BALL SLIGHTLY FORWARD USING FINGERTIP CONTROL AND LOWER ARM PUMPING ACTION.
3. DRIBBLE KNEE TO WAIST HIGH.
4. PROTECT BALL WITH ARM AND LEG.

Speed Dribble

Certain adjustments need to be made for executing a Speed Dribble effectively.

As the ball is dribbled, lean your body more forward and into the dribble. Control the ball from waist to chest level.

Keep your shoulders square to the direction of travel while protecting ball with your arm and leg.

1. **FROM BASIC DRIBBLE READY POSITION, LEAN FORWARD AND INTO DRIBBLE.**
2. **CONTROL BALL FROM WAIST- TO CHEST-HIGH.**

3. **KEEP SHOULDERS SQUARE TO DIRECTION OF TRAVEL.**
4. **PROTECT BALL WITH ARM AND LEG.**

changing directions

Reverse Pivot Change Techniques

From a Control Dribble, begin the *Reverse Pivot Change* by stopping temporarily on the foot opposite the dribbling hand. Legs are flexed at the knees with body weight slightly forward on the extended foot.

Pivot on balls of both feet while shifting weight to the extended foot. In making the pivot, transfer ball to the opposite hand. Now begin dribble, close to the floor as well as to the body.

Crossover Change Techniques

After learning the Control Dribble, develop methods of changing direction while dribbling. Execute the *Crossover Change* by bouncing the ball to the opposite hand. The shoulders are square to the direction of travel. Drive off the trailing leg and protect the ball with the free hand, arm and leg nearest opponent.

In reversing the ball from side to side, protect the ball with the arm and leg nearest your opponent.

1. **BEGIN CHANGE FROM CONTROL DRIBBLE.**
2. **STOP ON FOOT OPPOSITE DRIBBLING HAND.**
3. **PIVOT ON FRONT FOOT.**
4. **TRANSFER BALL TO OPPOSITE HAND.**
5. **COMPLETE PIVOT ON OPPOSITE FOOT.**
6. **PROTECT BALL WITH ARM AND LEG.**

1. **BEGIN CHANGE FROM CONTROL DRIBBLE.**
2. **BOUNCE BALL SHARPLY TO OPPOSITE HAND.**
3. **SQUARE SHOULDERS TO DIRECTION OF TRAVEL.**
4. **EXCHANGE MUST BE MADE QUICKLY SINCE BALL IS EXPOSED TO OPPONENT FOR BRIEF INSTANT.**
5. **DRIVE OFF TRAILING LEG.**
6. **PROTECT BALL WITH ARM AND LEG.**

Side View (Crossover Change Techniques)

passing

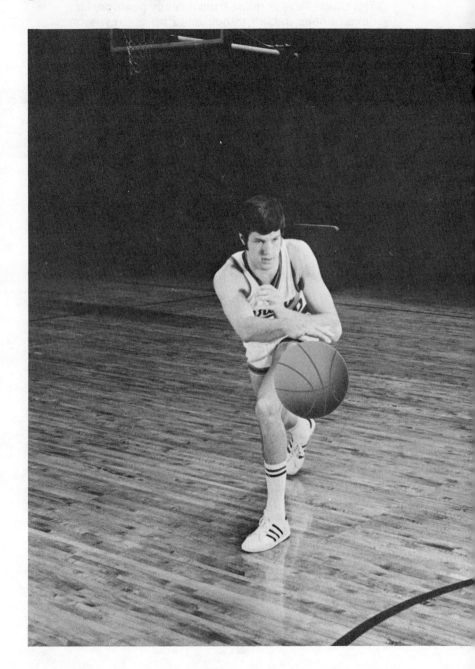

Chest Pass Techniques

The *Chest Pass* is made from a **ready position,** i.e., flexed knees, facing target, head up and eyes on intended receiver.

Ball is held at chest level with the hands placed above and slightly behind the center of the ball. Elbows are bent.

Grip the ball with the fingers and thumbs, keeping the palms of the hands off the ball.

Step to target and simultaneously execute a quick downward then upward motion with the hands to cock the wrists.

Uncock the wrists by pronating the wrists inward with the thumbs down. Keep the trajectory of the ball on a level plane.

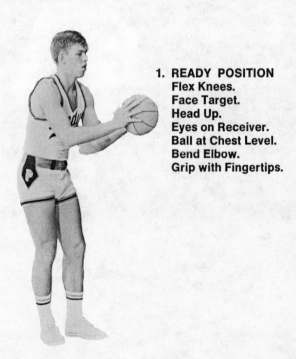

1. READY POSITION
Flex Knees.
Face Target.
Head Up.
Eyes on Receiver.
Ball at Chest Level.
Bend Elbow.
Grip with Fingertips.

2. STEP TO TARGET AND RELEASE BALL.
3. PRONATE WRISTS INWARD WITH THUMBS
   DOWN UPON RELEASE.

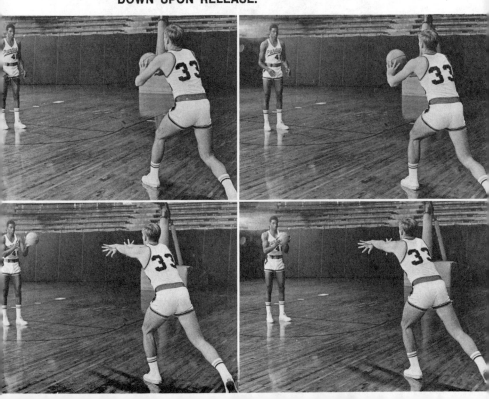

Two-Hand Bounce Pass

The *Two-Handed Bounce Pass* is merely a variation of the Chest Pass in that the ball is projected to the floor so that a teammate receives it after it has bounced once.

Otherwise all Chest Pass techniques apply.

1. **APPLY ALL CHEST PASS TECHNIQUES TO PROJECT BALL ON ONE BOUNCE TO TEAMMATE.**
2. **AVOID "TELEGRAPHING" PASS.**

One-Hand Flip Pass

This pass is sometimes referred to as a *Hook Pass* because such a pass is very often effective in getting the ball around a closely guarding defender.

Like the Chest Pass, the *One-Handed Flip Pass* may be delivered on a level trajectory or made to bounce once to a teammate. Often the bounce pass is the safer pass to make.

From the **ready position**, step out to the side of the defender where you intend to release the pass. With eyes on the receiver, grip the ball firmly in both hands until the point of release. Project the ball with the outside hand and pronate the wrist over the top of the ball to release the ball with a "flipping action."

1. FROM READY POSITION WITH EYES ON RECEIVER, STEP TO SIDE OF INTENDED PASS.
2. KEEP BOTH HANDS ON BALL UNTIL POINT OF RELEASE.
3. PRONATE WRIST OF OUTSIDE HAND OVER TOP OF BALL TO MAKE RELEASE WITH "FLIPPING ACTION."
4. DELIVER BALL ON LEVEL TRAJECTORY OR BOUNCE TO TEAMMATE.

One-Hand Flip Pass with Crossover Step

Some players prefer to execute a Hook Pass with a crossover step. Such a maneuver may be slightly more difficult to execute; however, it does provide greater protection in that the side of the body is turned to a tightly guarding defender. The shoulder, arm and leg are between the ball and defender, affording increased protection.

Overhead Pass Techniques

The *Overhead Pass* is also executed from a **ready position** which includes facing the target, head up, eyes on receiver, and gripping the ball with fingertips. Often, such a pass is made after a pivot to achieve a ready position.

From this position extend the arms upward, with the ball above and slightly in front of the head. Upon delivery step to target, simultaneously rotating, the

The mechanics of delivery are the same as for the One-Hand Flip Pass described before.

1. **TURN SIDE OF BODY TO DEFENDER BY STEPPING TO SIDE OF INTENDED PASS WITH CROSSOVER STEP.**

2. **SHOULDER, ARM AND LEG AFFORD PROTECTION BETWEEN DEFENDER AND BALL.**

3. **RELEASE BALL ON LEVEL TRAJECTORY OR BOUNCE TO TEAMMATE.**

fingers back and down to cock the wrists.

Uncock the wrists by pronating the wrists inward with thumbs down. The pass should be received approximately chest-high.

1. **READY POSITION: FACE TARGET WITH HEAD UP AND EYES ON RECEIVER. GRIP BALL WITH FINGERTIPS.**

2. **EXTEND ARMS UPWARD WITH BALL OVERHEAD. STEP TO TARGET.**

3. **PRONATE WRISTS INWARD, THUMBS DOWN.**

Baseball Pass Techniques

Such a pass is executed from the basic offensive stance very often after the passer has pivoted to face the receiver. A *Baseball Pass* may be thrown farther than any other pass; however, control and accuracy may be sacrificed if the pass is not made properly and prudently.

To throw this pass, draw the ball over your throwing shoulder and behind your ear. Extend your free arm toward the receiver while stepping out with the forward foot.

The ball is thrust forward while your weight is transferred from the back foot to the forward foot. Release the ball at full-arm extension as the leg on the throwing side comes forward to achieve a balanced follow-through. Note that the release is executed through fingertip control and wrist snap.

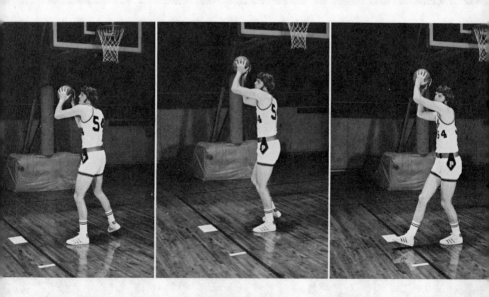

The free hand is proximate to the point of release should you decide to control the ball rather than throw the pass.

1. FROM READY POSITION, DRAW BALL OVER THROWING SHOULDER AND BEHIND EAR.

2. EXTEND FREE ARM TOWARD RECEIVER AND STEP FORWARD.

3. TRANSFER WEIGHT FROM BACK FOOT TO FORWARD FOOT AND RELEASE BALL AT FULL-ARM EXTENSION.

4. BRING BACK LEG FORWARD, INTO BALANCED FOLLOW-THROUGH POSITION.

5. FINGERTIP CONTROL AND WRIST SNAP ARE ESSENTIAL ELEMENTS FOR EFFECTIVE PASS.

6. FREE HAND PROXIMATE TO BALL SHOULD YOU DECIDE NOT TO CONTINUE WITH THROW.

drive to the basket

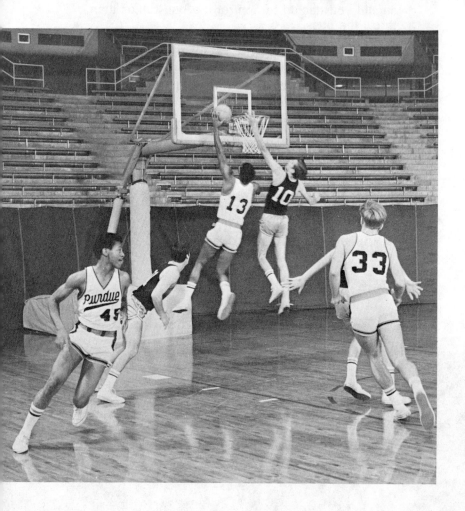

Receiving the Ball from a Teammate

The player who moves well without the ball and is constantly on the move most often gets free for a pass from a teammate.

Usually the most effective means of receiving a pass is to take a couple of steps toward the passer. In so doing the receiver reduces the distance and time which the defender has to intercept the ball. However, faking toward the passer or to one side, then reversing in the opposite direction, also may provide an opportunity to receive a pass safely.

1. **MOVE TO GET CLEAR FOR A PASS FROM A TEAMMATE.**
2. **STEPPING TOWARD PASSER CUTS DOWN DISTANCE AND TIME WHICH DEFENDER HAS TO INTERCEPT BALL.**
3. **KEEP EYE ON BALL, MAKE CATCH AND SET UP TO MAKE A PASS, SHOT OR DRIBBLE AND DRIVE TO BASKET.**

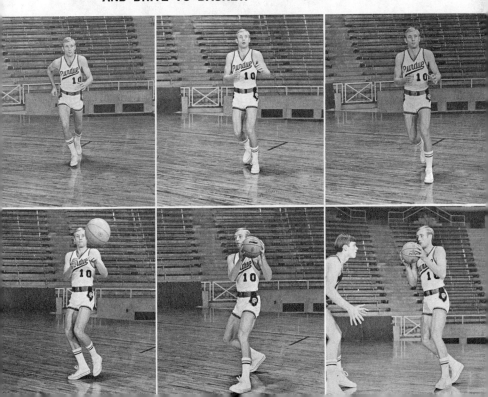

Drive Techniques

Go to meet ball, pivot to face basket and assume a **ready position,** i.e., head up, knees flexed and eyes focused on surrounding action plus ball.

Fake in opposite direction of the intended drive, pull ball across body, and with the foot opposite the fake explode with a lead step past the defender. The ball is projected forward and to the side of the dribbling hand. Simultaneously drive opposite foot forward to continue the penetration of the drive. Protect the ball with arm and leg nearest the defender.

Crossover Drive Techniques

Go to meet ball, pivot to face basket and assume a **ready position.**

Fake in opposite direction of the intended drive, pull ball across body and, using a crossover step with foot on the side of the fake, explode past the defender.

As the ball is projected forward and to the side of the dribbling hand, drive opposite foot forward to continue penetration of the drive. Protect the ball with arm and leg nearest the defender.

1. FEINT OPPONENT OFF BALANCE.

2. PULL BALL ACROSS BODY.

3. DRIVE OPPOSITE FOOT FORWARD.

4. CONTINUE PENETRATION.

1. FAKE IN DIRECTION OPPOSITE INTENDED DRIVE.

2. SHIFT WEIGHT TO OPPOSITE FOOT, PULL BALL ACROSS BODY AND BEGIN CROSSOVER STEP.

3. CROSS OVER WITH LEAD FOOT.

4. DRIVE TRAILING FOOT FORWARD. CONTINUE PENETRATION. PROTECT BALL WITH ARM AND LEG.

shooting

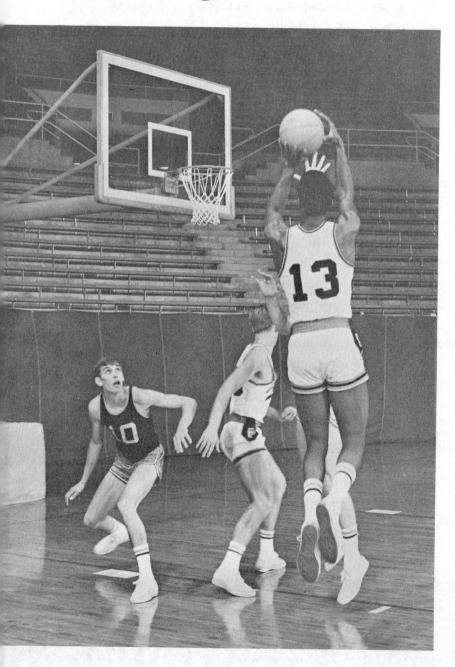

Lay-Up Shot Techniques

The *Lay-Up* is probably the most basic shot in basketball. When shooting a Lay-Up, the head is up and the eyes are focused at a point on the backboard where the ball is to be banked into the basket.

To achieve the shooting position, shift your weight to the foot opposite the shooting hand. Explode off the extended front foot, then drive the opposite leg upward.

During the drive upward, carry the ball in both hands to a point above and in front of the head. Release the ball to the shooting hand and extend the shooting arm fully. The palm of the shooting hand should face the basket while the ball is controlled with the fingertips.

At the release, place the ball gently against the backboard and pronate the wrist inward on the follow-through.

1. HEAD UP WITH EYES ON BACKBOARD.
2. SHIFT WEIGHT TO FRONT FOOT.
3. EXPLODE OFF FRONT FOOT; DRIVE
   OTHER LEG FORWARD AND UPWARD.

4. **EXTEND SHOOTING ARM FULLY AND CONTROL BALL WITH FINGERTIPS.**
5. **WITH PALM FACING BACKBOARD, RELEASE BALL AGAINST BACKBOARD.**
6. **PRONATE WRIST ON FOLLOW-THROUGH.**

Crossover Lay-Up Shot

As your drive approaches the basket, execute the techniques of the Crossover Change Dribble to bring the dribble under control as you rotate the shoulders and square your body to the board.

Jump off the extended inside foot and bring the ball up with both hands, extending your arms to the point of release. Pronate the wrist and shooting hand inward upon release of the ball to the board.

1. **AS DRIVE APPROACHES BASKET, EXECUTE CROSSOVER CHANGE DRIBBLE.**
2. **ROTATE SHOULDERS AND SQUARE BODY TO BOARD.**
3. **JUMP OFF EXTENDED INSIDE FOOT.**
4. **WITH BALL IN BOTH HANDS, EXTEND ARMS TO POINT OF RELEASE.**
5. **PRONATE WRIST AND SHOOTING HAND INWARD UPON RELEASE OF BALL TO BOARD.**

Inside Power Shot Techniques

The *Inside Power Shot* is executed from a **ready position**, i.e., head up, knees flexed, and eyes focused at a point on the backboard where the ball is to be banked into the basket.

Take a lead step with foot nearest the basket. As step is taken, bounce the ball in front of the body midway between the feet. Then close the stance by bringing the rear foot forward. Simultaneously drop the center of gravity for upward jump.

Explode off both feet upward and laterally to the basket. At the same time, carry the ball upward with both hands to a point above and in front of the head. Extend the body and shooting arm fully.

Release the ball to the fingertips of the shooting hand with the palm facing the backboard. Protect the shot with the free arm and complete the shot by pronating the wrist inward on follow-through.

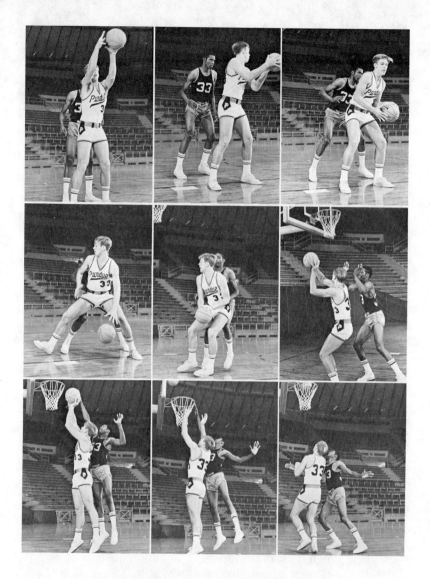

1. **FROM READY POSITION, TAKE LEAD STEP TO TARGET.**
2. **DROP CENTER OF GRAVITY.**
3. **BRING FEET TOGETHER; CONTROL BALL WITH BOTH HANDS.**
4. **EXPLODE UP AND EXTEND BODY FULLY.**
5. **PROTECT SHOT WITH FREE ARM.**
6. **RELEASE BALL AGAINST BACKBOARD.**

Jump Shot Techniques

The *Jump Shot* is made from a **ready position**, i.e., head up, eyes on basket and weight distributed on the balls of the feet, with the foot on the side of the shooting hand extended slightly.

Before and during the jump, the ball is controlled by both hands. Place the hand opposite the shooting hand on the side and slightly behind the center of the ball. The shooting hand is placed behind the ball.

While exploding upward, carry the ball to the shooting position with both hands. The shooting arm forms a 90-degree angle, and the eyes are focused on the basket.

Make the release when the shooting arm is at a full extension and at the peak of the jump. On the release, control the shot with the fingertips and follow through by pronating the wrist forward.

1. **READY POSITION**
   Face Basket with Head Up. Flex Knees with Weight on Balls of Feet. Control Ball with Both Hands.
2. **EXPLODE UP WITH EYES ON RIM.**
3. **SHOOTING ARM FORMS 90-DEGREE ANGLE.**
4. **EXTEND ARM FULLY ON RELEASE.**

5. CONTROL SHOT WITH FINGERTIPS.
6. PRONATE WRIST ON FOLLOW-THROUGH.

Turnaround Jump Shot Techniques

The *Turnaround Jump Shot* has all the basic shooting techniques of the Jump Shot.

The fundamental differences of the Turnaround Jump Shot are: The shooter's back is to the basket when receiving the ball. The feet are parallel rather than one foot slightly forward as in the jump shot. A pivot must be made to place the shooter in position to make the shot.

Once facing the basket, all jump shot techniques apply.

1. READY POSITION
   Back to Basket with Head Up. Flex Knees with
   Feet Parallel. Weight on Balls of Feet.
2. PIVOT TO FACE BASKET.

3. CONTROL BALL WITH BOTH HANDS.
4. EXPLODE UP. SHOOTING ARM FORMS 90-DEGREE ANGLE. EYES ON RIM.
5. EXTEND ARM FULLY ON RELEASE. CONTROL SHOT WITH FINGERTIPS. PRONATE WRIST ON FOLLOW-THROUGH.

Side View (Turnaround Jump Shot)

One-Hand Set Shot Techniques

The *One-Hand Set Shot* is most commonly used at the free-throw line although it may be shot effectively around the perimeter of the keyhole.

Execute this shot from the basic offensive stance while holding the ball in front of your face, just below eye level for purposes of "sighting."

The shooting hand should be placed behind and slightly off the ball's center with the support hand placed on the side.

Initial body movement is very important in executing this shot. In one continuous motion this sequence develops: 1) knees flex slightly, 2) body (trunk) flexes at waist, 3) ball is brought down toward chin as wrist cocks, 4) ball is pushed toward basket with release coming at point of full arm extension (wrists flex) and 5) hand and wrists continue to flex on follow-through to basket.

From beginning to end, your body weight moves slightly forward to the balls of your feet. Body rhythm is all-important in executing this shot to the point of release from the fingertips.

1. **FROM BASIC OFFENSIVE STANCE, HOLD BALL IN FRONT OF FACE JUST BELOW EYE LEVEL. EYES FOCUS ON RIM.**
2. **FLEX KNEES, BEND BODY AT WAIST.**
3. **BRING BALL TOWARD CHIN AS YOU COCK WRIST.**
4. **PUSH BALL TOWARD BASKET, MAKING RELEASE AT FULL-ARM EXTENSION. CONTROL BALL WITH FINGERTIPS.**
5. **PRONATE HAND AND WRIST ON RELEASE AND FOLLOW-THROUGH.**

Hook Shot Techniques

From a **ready position** with your back toward the basket, start your move by taking a lead step toward the takeoff point for the shot.

Rotate the body and shift your weight to the lead foot as you carry the ball upward to the point of release. Note that the ball is carried with shooting hand slightly underneath. Use the opposite hand to control the ball toward release point and protect the shot thereafter.

Jump off the lead foot (inside) and raise the opposite knee and leg upward to carry your body momentum toward the target.

The release is made as the ball is carried up in an arc toward the basket and the shooting arm extends out to the point where the ball leaves the fingertips. Your hand and wrist then rotate over the ball in line with the release on follow-through.

1. TAKE LEAD STEP TOWARD RELEASE
   POINT.
2. JUMP OFF INSIDE FOOT WHILE
   CARRYING BALL UPWARD WITH
   BOTH HANDS.
3. DRIVE OUTSIDE KNEE AND LEG
   UPWARD TO PROJECT BODY
   MOMENTUM TOWARD TARGET.

4. ARCH BALL TOWARD BASKET AND EXTEND SHOOTING ARM TO POINT OF RELEASE. PROTECT BALL WITH FREE HAND.

5. RELEASE BALL OFF FINGERTIPS AND ROTATE HAND OVER BALL IN LINE WITH RELEASE ON FOLLOW-THROUGH.

rebounding

Blocking Out for Rebounds

Certainly one of the most important fundamentals in the game of basketball is blocking out for rebounds. The *block-out* is executed as soon as the offensive player can diagnose and intercept the offensive player's route to the basket.

The actual block-out is the result of the defensive man's executing either a **front pivot** or a **reverse pivot** which in effect blocks the oponent's path to the rebound.

Use the pivot which suits the situation best and the one which you can confidently and properly execute.

As soon as a shot attempt is detected, determine immediately what path the offensive player will take toward the basket. Pivot to intercept his move and into a ready position for the rebound. The pivot affords you an advantageous inside position for the rebound.

1. IMMEDIATELY AFTER SHOT IS ATTEMPTED, DETERMINE WHAT PATH "YOUR MAN" WILL TAKE TOWARD THE BASKET.
2. USE PIVOT WHICH SUITS THE SITUATION AND YOU BEST.
3. PIVOT INSIDE, TOWARD THE OFFENSIVE PLAYER ON THE FRONT PIVOT.

4. OR, PIVOT OUTSIDE, SLIGHTLY AWAY FROM
   THE OFFENSIVE PLAYER FOR REVERSE PIVOT.
5. SET UP IN READY POSITION FOR REBOUND.

Rebounding Techniques

With the body in a **ready position**, i.e., head up, knees flexed, eyes on backboard, arms above the waist and feet parallel, drop center of gravity and explode upward to full extension.

In rebounding the ball use a firm grip with fingers spread. Pull the ball to chest level with elbows out. Upon landing, the feet should be at least a shoulder's-width apart with knees flexed.

1. **READY POSITION**
   Head Up. Eyes on Ball. Arm above Waist. Knees Flexed. Feet Parallel. Weight on Balls of Feet.

2. **DROP CENTER OF GRAVITY AND EXPLODE UP, EXTENDING ARMS.**
3. **EXTEND BODY FULLY, GRIP BALL WITH FINGERS SPREAD.**
4. **PULL BALL TO CHEST.**
5. **FLEX KNEES ON LANDING WITH FEET A SHOULDER'S-WIDTH APART.**

Outlet Pass

From the landing position quickly pivot for an outlet pass. A Chest, Overhead or Baseball Pass is most often thrown. With a teammate nearby, a quick Flip Pass may be effective.

A quick and accurate *outlet pass* is important to get the ball down floor to set up the offense before the opponents can recover.

6. **PIVOT OUTSIDE FOR OUTLET PASS.**

Basketball Court Diagram

Provided through the courtesy of the National Federation of State High School Athletic Associations. *(Diagram 2)*

rules simplified

The Playing Area

Basketball may be played indoors or out-of-doors, although in America the game is generally played indoors. Basketball is played on a court ranging in size from a maximum of 94 feet long by 50 feet wide to a minimum of 74 feet long by 42 feet wide. Ideal measurements are:

COLLEGE AGE   **94 by 50 feet**

HIGH SCHOOL AGE **84 by 50 feet**

The court is to have a hard surface usually of wood. There should be at least three feet (preferably ten feet) of unobstructed space on all sides of the court.

At either end of the court are backboards made of wood, glass, steel or other rigid, flat materials. The backboards must be one of two types: a rectangular board six feet long and four feet high, or a fan-shaped board. The front face of the backboard is to be four feet from the end boundary line, and parallel. The basket is attached to the center of the backboard so that the rim of the basket is ten feet from the floor. From the basket ring is suspended a white cord net.

In the exact center of the court is a circle, four feet in diameter, known as the *center circle*. A "restraining circle," 12 feet in diameter, is concentric outside the center circle.

In the center at each end of the court is a *free-throw lane,* 12 feet wide, ending in circles 12 feet in diameter. The centers of these circles are to be 19 feet from the end boundary lines. A *free-throw line* is drawn through the circle, parallel with the end boundary line. The free throw line is 15 feet from the plane of the face of the backboard.

A *division line* divides the court into two equal parts. A team's *front court* is that part of the court containing the team's own basket, that is, the basket through which a team tries to score its points. The other half of the court is known as that team's *backcourt.* For the opposing team, the names are reversed.

The Ball

A basketball is to be round, no larger than 30 inches in circumference and no smaller than 29 inches. Its weight should be no more than 22 ounces nor less than 20 ounces. When inflated, it should bounce to a height (measured to top of ball) of not less than 49 inches nor more than 54 inches after it has been dropped from a height of six feet (measured to bottom of ball). The home team is to provide the game ball.

The Team

A basketball team consists of five players, generally known as a *center,* two *forwards* and two *guards.* A team cannot begin a game with less than five players, but if it has no substitutes to replace disqualified players, it must finish the game with less than five players. A player must leave the game after committing five personal fouls, and cannot return during that game. Each player must wear a numbered shirt.

The Officials

The officials should be a *referee* and an *umpire,* assisted by two *timers* and two *scorers.* A single timer and a single scorer may be used if acceptable to both teams. Officials must conduct the game according to the rules.

Scorers record personal and technical fouls, and notify the referee when the fifth personal foul is called on a player. They also record time-outs charged against each team. In scoring, most scorers use the following symbols:

P1, P2, P3, etc. for personal fouls;

T for technical fouls;

O for free throw attempt, X inside O if try is good;

2 for field goals.

Note: See page 74 for description of fouls.

A field goal counts two points. A successful free throw counts one point.

Game Times

College teams play two 20-minute halves, with a 15-minute intermission between the halves.

Teams of high school age play four eight-minute quarters, with two one-minute intermissions between the quarters and a ten-minute intermission between the halves.

Overtime Periods

If the score is tied at the end of the second half in college games, play shall continue for an extra period of five minutes, or for as many extra five-minute periods as are needed to break the tie. A one-minute intermission is taken before each extra period. The ball is put in play in the center circle at the start of each extra period.

High school games which end in ties are played off in extra periods of three minutes each, with a two-minute intermission before each extra period. A team wins when it is ahead by one point or more at the end of any extra period. The first team to lead by two points during the second extra period wins the game.

Time-outs

Each team is allowed five charged time-outs during regular play. A charged time-out is either a time-out requested by a player when the ball is dead or that player's team has control of the ball; or a time-out for an injury or removal of a disqualified player. A time-out is not charged if an injured or disqualified player is replaced within 1½ minutes. If the officials halt a game to permit a player to tie a shoelace, a time-out is not charged.

Some Other Rules

Visiting teams have the choice of baskets for the first half. Teams change baskets for the second half.

The score of a forfeited game is 2 to 0.

When a team gains control of the basketball in its back-court, it must move the ball into its front court within ten seconds, unless the ball is touched by an opponent. When the ball is touched, a new play starts, and a new ten-second period is allowed.

Common Offensive Alignments

In developing team play many factors must be taken into consideration before settling upon any one offensive alignment. The alignment used is merely a vehicle whereby the team may execute certain movements which best utilize the individual talents of the team and express the philosophy of the coach. In certain strategic situations the offensive alignment is a countermove to specific defenses.

Most common offensive alignments utilize a single post situation, that is, with one pivotman playing close to the basket or no further away from the hoop than the foul line.

SINGLE LOW POST OFFENSIVE SETUP.
This alignment is sometimes referred to as a *2-3 offense.*
1 and **2** are guards, **3** and **4** forwards and **5** is the center or pivotman. *(Diagram 3)*

Key to diagrams
on page 77.

SINGLE HIGH POST OFFENSIVE SETUP.
This alignment is sometimes referred to as a *2-1-2 offense.*
The positions correspond to those of Diagram 3. *(Diagram 4)*

TANDEM OR 1-3-1 OFFENSIVE SETUP. In this alignment positions are referred to by different terms. **1** is the point, **2** and **3** are wings, **4** is the *high post* and **5** is the *low post*. This setup is very popular vs certain zone defenses. *(Diagram 5)*

DOUBLE POST OFFENSIVE SETUP. Sometimes referred to as a *3-2 alignment*. Players **1**, **2** and **3** are perimeter or a combination of guards and quick forwards. **4** and **5** are low post players. *(Diagram 6)*

Comparing the positions within the various offensive alignments, two important factors must be observed when considering placement of personnel: 1) the distance from the basket, and 2) whether the position requires facing the basket or back to basket.

Certain characteristics and skills are required for proficiency at each position. There is some obvious overlapping within the various types of alignments.

Guards (Small Perimeter Players)

Guards are usually the smaller of the three positions: however, size is a definite advantage if the other necessary attributes are present. Speed, quickness and agility are the most important of the physical qualities for this position. Necessary skills are: ball handling (dribbling and passing,) play-making and outside shooting. Personnel at this position are also referred to as "floor generals" or "quarterbacks" because of their importance as team leaders on the floor. In the 1-3-1 setup they are pointmen (Diagram **5**)

Forwards (Large Perimeter Players)

Forwards or cornermen, sometimes a wing as in the 1-3-1, must possess many of the same qualities as the small perimeter players, but size is much more important because of their added responsi-bility as rebounders. Physical attributes necessary are height, strength, quickness and agility. Neces-sary skills include rebounding, passing and receiv-ing, outside and corner shooting and ball handling for driving.

Pivotmen (High or Low Post)

Centers or pivotmen occupy the post positions which require back-to-the-basket offensive skills.

Necessary skills include inside shooting around the basket, rebounding and passing. Obviously, most important of the physical requirements are height, strength, ability to jump and mobility in traffic.

Basic Individual Offensive Maneuvers

Certain individual basketball skills are just as necessary as the aforementioned physical attributes and simple skills or fundamentals.

Recommended for all face-to-the-basket ball players is mastery of at least two or three of the following offensive maneuvers.

1. **FAKE RIGHT THEN DRIVE LEFT.**
   FAKE LEFT THEN DRIVE RIGHT.

2. **FAKE RIGHT, LEFT THEN DRIVE RIGHT.**
   FAKE LEFT, RIGHT THEN DRIVE LEFT.

3. **FAKE RIGHT (HESITATE) THEN DRIVE RIGHT.**
   FAKE LEFT (HESITATE) THEN DRIVE LEFT.

4. **ROCKER STEP FAKE AND DRIVE RIGHT.**
   ROCKER STEP FAKE AND DRIVE LEFT.

5. **FAKE SHOT AND DRIVE RIGHT.**
   FAKE SHOT AND DRIVE LEFT.

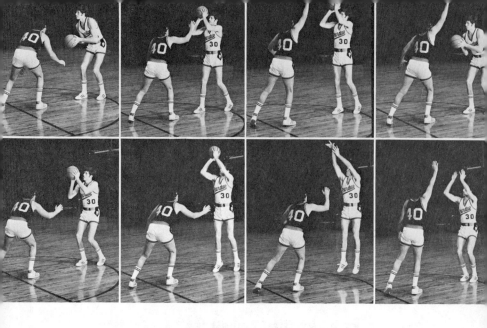

6. FAKE SHOT, BACK TO READY POSITION THEN SHOOT.

All postmen should develop at least two or three of the following back-to-the-basket maneuvers:

1. FAKE RIGHT, COME BACK LEFT AND SHOOT.
   FAKE LEFT, COME BACK RIGHT AND SHOOT.

2. FAKE RIGHT, HOOK BACK WITH LEFT FOOT AND SHOOT.
   FAKE LEFT, HOOK BACK WITH RIGHT FOOT AND SHOOT.

3. FAKE RIGHT, PAUSE THEN GO RIGHT.
   FAKE LEFT, PAUSE THEN GO LEFT.

4. FAKE RIGHT, COME BACK TO RIGHT WITH LEFT FOOT (FORWARD PIVOT). USE CROSS-OVER STEP AND SHOOT.
   FAKE LEFT, COME BACK TO RIGHT WITH LEFT FOOT (FORWARD PIVOT). USE CROSS-OVER STEP AND SHOOT.

5. REVERSE PIVOT, FAKE RIGHT AND GO LEFT.
REVERSE PIVOT, FAKE LEFT AND GO RIGHT.

Basic Two- and Three-Man Offensive Maneuvers

For the most part, the game of basketball is developed around individual skills of the team; however, for the sake of teamwork and organization, team offenses are structured around a few basic two- or three-man "games" or movements. The following maneuvers are designed to set up quick scoring opportunities and stay within the framework of team play.

Key to diagrams
on page 77.

GIVE AND GO MANEUVER.
1 passes to **2**, sets up his defensive man with one or two steps toward **2** (as if to go and receive return handoff) then sharply breaks for the basket. **2** anticipates the move and makes a good lead pass to **1**.
(Diagram 7)

PICK AND ROLL MANEUVER.

1 dribbles at **2's** inside shoulder forcing his defender to go behind the pick by **2**. As **1** dribbles off **2**, **2** pivots on inside foot screening off the defender to chase **1** and force a defensive switch. **1** passes to **2** who then releases for the basket. *(Diagram 8)*

GUARD AROUND MANEUVER.

1 passes to **2**, makes a good jab-step fake, then breaks around **2** (brushing off defender). **2** pivots on inside foot and makes overhead pass to **1** cutting to basket. *(Diagram 9)*

SCREEN AWAY MANEUVER.

1 passes to **3** and moves away from pass to set a screen on **2's** defender. **2** must time his cutoff, **1** allowing him to get into proper screen position, then, setting his man up, break off **1's** block to receive pass from **3**.
(Diagram 10)

HANDOFF W/RELEASE MANEUVER.

1 passes to **3**, sets his man up with a fake away from the ball then goes behind **3** to receive handback. **3** releases away and sets up in a low post position. **1** then passes to **3**. *(Diagram 11)*

LOW POST SCREEN MANEUVER.

Using the same idea as indicated in Diagram **10** the screen away can be set to free the low post by **1** blocking **5's** defender. **3** makes pass to **5** as he breaks open around screen. *(Diagram 12)*

GUARD-GUARD SPLIT OFF POST MANEUVER.

1 passes to **5** in high post. **1** goes immediately to set an inside brush screen on **2's** defensive man. **2's** cut and **1's** release occur at the same instant, creating the split action off **5**. *(Diagram 13)*

SIDE SPLIT OFF POST MANEUVER.
1 passes to 3 and sets up his man while 3 makes pass into post to 5. 3 comes and sets an inside brush screen for 1. 1's cut and 3's release occur at the same instant, creating the split action off 5. *(Diagram 14)*

Defense—Types, Theories and Skills of Play

Team defense is divided into two basic types, **man-to-man** and **zone**. A third type being used more and more today is a combination of man-to-man and zone, but it is used for special situations almost exclusively.

Coaching philosophies will vary to some degree. Basically, however, the man-to-man defense is oriented primarily toward individual player for player assignments, sometimes referred to as match-ups. Zone defenses are more oriented to ball and area of the court. Both defenses rely upon weakside (away from the ball) basket coverage based upon direction of ball movement.

In the various zone defensive alignments, players are assigned specific areas to defend whenever the ball enters their area. In the **combination defense**, usually one player will be assigned in a one-on-one man match-up while the remaining four will form a four-man zone (box or diamond). Sometimes if there is a need to defend two players on a man-to-man basis, the remaining three men will form a triangle zone.

It is most common for both basic types of defenses (man and zone) to be played with varying degrees of pressure as well as extending coverages from normal halfcourt to mid-court, three-quarter, or full-court presses. As with the selection of offensive alignments and styles of play, the same basic factors influence the selection of team defense or defenses to be employed. The quality of individual talent and coaching philosophy are weighed very heavily in determining the approach to team defense.

All factors being equal, most coaches feel that the man-to-man defense played as intended gives the best total coverage to the problems posed by the opponent's offensive strengths. Philosophies may vary for various reasons as already pointed out and for that reason as well as certain game strategies which may apply, either defense may be played very aggressively or, in varying degrees, very passively.

Basic to proper individual execution of either defense is the mastering of the fundamentals required. It is most important to develop proper defensive position with the body in a semi-crouch position with knees flexed, back straight, head up and with arms and hands comfortably spread. The feet are probably the single most important aspect of good defensive play. They must be kept spread approximately a shoulder's-width apart with a slightly staggered stance and weight primarily over the balls of the feet. The player must guard against crossing the feet with any movement and should concentrate on short, quick shifts of foot position to maintain good position defensively.

Guarding a man without the ball is a very important aspect of man defense. Anticipation of his movements, avoiding picks or screens and **preventing him from receiving the ball**, all will take hours of drilling to perfect. Communication is a must between players. All sound defensive players are alert and ready to help by talking to their teammates. With only a few exceptions the basic rule for man-to-man defense is to stay between your man and the basket, control his attempt to drive and not let him have a good percentage shot.

Like offensive alignments, there are many variations of zone defenses. Most common are: 2-1-2, 2-3,

1-3-1, 1-2-2 and the 3-2. Additionally, there are several half-court and full-court zone presses. Size, quickness and jumping (rebounding) ability are the prime factors in selecting the placement of personnel for defensive assignments within each zone defense. Usually these defensive position assignments closely parallel the same offensive positions. In some cases, coaches may make strategic changes or "adjustments."

In Diagram **15** the basic 2-3 zone positions are shown. The subsequent diagrams show each man's adjustment (rules of coverage) with the movement of the ball around the perimeter and into the corner.

2-3 ZONE DEFENSE COVERAGE.
Shown when the ball is out front at a normal guard position. If the offense does not provide a normal match-up for the defense, then players start to cheat in the anticipated direction of ball movement. *(Diagram 15)*

Key to diagrams
on page 77.

CONTINUING THE 2-3 COVERAGE.
As the ball is passed from **1** to **3**. X_1 goes to cover **3**, X_3 will temporarily hold until X_1 can get there, then release back. X_5 plays in line with the ball and the hoop. X_2 plays in line with the ball and the midpoint of the foul line. X_4 plays in line with the ball and the corner opposite the ball. *(Diagram 16)*

CONTINUING THE 2-3 COVERAGE.

... as 3 passes to 5 in the corner, X_3 covers 5, X_1 drops off 3 back toward basket two or three steps to prevent pass from 5 to 4. X_2 plays in line with ball and midpoint of foul line. X_5 plays in line with ball and the hoop. X_4 plays in line with the ball and the corner opposite ball. *(Diagram 17)*

Illustrating the two popular combination zone defenses, Diagram **18** shows the box-and-one with the man-to-man "Chaser" X_1 on **3**.

BOX-AND-ONE DEFENSE.

In this alignment defender X_1 simply tries to guard 3 as closely as possible. X_2, X_3, X_4 and X_5 play a box zone. *(Diagram 18)*

Diagram **19** shows the same situation as in Diagram **18**, except the four remaining players align in a diamond zone defense.

DIAMOND-AND-ONE DEFENSE.

The theory of defense in the diamond is identical to that of the box. Individual responsibilities are the same; however, the shifts for the box differ slightly from the diamond. *(Diagram 19)*

To be effective, zone defenses must function as a precision unit with all five men reacting to their assigned areas of coverage simultaneously. Good players within zone defenses know their assignment and react instinctively. Again, as in the man-to-man defense, it is most important for players to communicate at all times and always maintain good defensive positions for quick movement or shifts in position.

Editor's Note About Behind the Back Dribbles, Between the Legs Dribbles, Behind the Back Passes, etc.

Techniques presented in this book are those felt by the consultants to be fundamental to the success of any basketball team regardless of age. In recent years, more teams have begun to use such skills as the *Behind the Back Pass* and *Cross-Behind Dribble Change* which have become more widespread.

While the consultants necessarily do not discourage the use of these techniques, they do point out that such tactics need be suited to the age and skills of the team members involved. While some players become very proficient in employing such techniques, others run into considerable difficulty when attempting to do so.

Therefore, such techniques have not been described in this book since they are not considered basic to successful play.

Ball-Handling Drills

Obviously, ball handling is one of the most basic of all basketball fundamentals. The following drills are designed to develop an individual's skill in this area. Specifically, eye-hand co-ordination, hand and finger strength, and speed and rhythm with the hands are direct values derived from regular practice through these drills. Naturally, as a player develops himself in these skill aspects, he also gains self-confidence, so necessary to successful athletic competition.

The following exercises constitute a normal practice routine:

As a preface to all drills, start by slapping the ball into the receiving hand rather than merely placing it there. This will develop hand and finger strength.

The starting position for the body is shown at the left. Player should assume a semi-crouched position with the ball in front of his body at knee level. For the first two exercises the feet should be spread a shoulder's-width.
Exercise 1

Single Leg Circle
In this exercise the player circles one leg at a time with the ball. Both legs should be circled for the complete drill. Start with the ball in the right hand in front of the body, pass the ball and bring it around the left leg to front position and into right hand. Continue this movement around one leg, then stop and start around the other leg, starting the movement with the left hand passing the ball back between the legs and circling the right leg.
Exercise 2

Figure "8"

Starting as in the previous exercise, keep the ball in the left hand and put it between the legs to where the right hand can receive it. The right hand then passes the ball around the right leg and back through between the legs to the left hand. Always be sure to start the ball from in front, through the legs. *Exercise 3*

Around Both Legs and Body

Assume a slightly greater crouched position than in the first two exercises. Bring feet close together and in this crouched position, carry the ball around the left side with the left hand to the right hand and then around to the front again. Change directions whenever you wish. Start with a ball around the ankles, then move it up around the knees, then straighten the body to an erect position and pass the ball around the waist. Bend over and lower the ball back down around the knees and then the ankles and back up and so on. *Exercise 4*

Speed Drill (Figure "8" with Drop)

Use the same body position as in Exercises **1** and **2**. Start this exercise as a regular Figure "8" but, when bringing the ball around the left leg with the left hand, do not put the ball between the legs, but swing it on around in front and to the right which then carries the ball around the right leg and through the legs from the back side. Bring the ball to the left hand, then merely drop the ball to the court and quickly exchange hand positions by bringing the right arm around in front and putting the left arm to the rear. Grasp the ball with both hands as it bounces up and continue the maneuver. *Exercise 5*

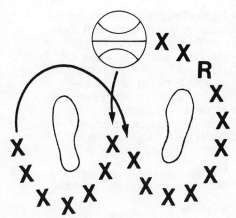

Figure "8" Dribble (Stationary)

Use the same positions as for Exercise **2**, only this time dribble the ball with the Figure "8" pathway. Keep the ball low on the dribble. Feet may assume a slightly wide base and body may lean in the direction of the dribble.

Exercise 6

Fingertips Up and Down the Body

Keep elbows stiff. Start with the ball out in front of the body at arm's length while standing erect. Tap the ball from one hand to the other as you move it above the head and down to the knees in a gradual movement. Keep your elbows stiff. When controlling the ball over the head, shuffle the feet from side to side. The "shuffle" shifts body weight from leg to leg without crossing the feet.

Exercise 7

Crab Run—Putting Ball Through Legs

Assume a crouched-running position and start with an exaggerated long stride run. As you step out with the right leg, place the ball under that thigh with a left-hand to right-hand movement. Then, as the left leg comes up and forward, use a right-hand to left-hand movement to pass the ball under the left thigh. Continue on down the court as fast as you can with this drill. Ball makes the same movement as in the stationary Figure "8" Drill. *Exercise 8*

Zigzag Dribble Between Legs

Begin dribbling to the right, then dribble the ball under the right leg (on the forward step) with a low sharp bounce crossing over and into the left hand. Immediately change direction of body movement to the left (as diagramed) and execute the same crossover bounce under the left leg on the third dribble in that direction.

Work for greater maneuverability and more speed as you improve.

Exercise 9

Basic Conditioning and Fundamental Drills

Tapping Against Backboard

- Tap on both sides of the backboard with left and right hand respectively 15 times each. Begin the drill by throwing the ball up to the board and tapping the ball a minimum of three times before tipping it into the basket. Keep your arm fully extended when making a tap and keep the ball controlled off the fingertips. Coninuous jumping will help develop the legs and body co-ordination.

Jump Shooting

- Practice your jump shooting facing the basket by taking a quick dribble or two both to your left and to your right for the jump shot. Concentrate on making your shooting motion one continuous smooth movement. Get up to the height of your jump before releasing the shot. Make sure that the free hand is used to support the ball until the split-second of release of shot. Make your release at the height of your jump.

- Have a friend rebound your shot and throw it out to you. Receive the pass, maintain body control, stop and jump-shoot. It is extremely important to be able to receive a pass on the run, stop and execute a jump shot properly. Receive the pass, stop under control, jump and release your shot toward the basket. Come down, make a fake in the opposite direction with a quick jab step, turn and break hard to an area approximately 10 to 15 feet in the opposite direction to receive your next pass. Stop and repeat the same shooting maneuver as described. Do this until you have made 15 baskets. Change the areas in which you practice often.

Foul Shooting

- Concentrate on proper mechanics and body rhythm for release of the shot. It is recommended that you step back from the free-throw line and establish a new foot position with each shot.

Defensive Footwork Maneuvers

- Assume the defensive position to get into a good, naturally comfortable stance with one foot slightly in front of the other and weight evenly distributed over both feet, primarily on the balls of the feet. Get your hands in a good defensive position and keep them fairly close to your body. From this position, start your boxer shuffle. Shuffle without crossing your feet at any time. First, make your movement to the left, then back to your right. Change direction by going forward, backward left, right, forward and backward. This is excellent for your footwork and for your body balance. Make sure your steps are short and quick in your movement.

Defensive Retreating Drill

- Start from the defensive position already described by turning in and running four or five steps. Then roll the lead foot back across the body and make a complete pivot turn while you are running. This is good for body balance and co-ordination when running in a defensive position.

Change of Direction-Triangle Drill

- Note the five numbers below (Diagram **20**) and set up this situation on a court so that approximately 5 to 6 feet are between each point (number). Assume the defensive position already described above.

  From point 1, start your movement with a defensive slide (keeping your face forward) toward number 2. Once you reach point 2, immediately react forward, coming up on a defender with the ball to point 3, then react back in a defensive slide back to point 1. Continue this maneuver moving to point 4, back to point 5 then up to point 1 again. This should be repeated a series of five or six times without stopping. Work for quickness, keeping the body in proper defensive position throughout the drill.

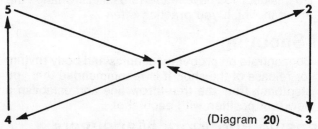

(Diagram **20**)

Basic Passing

- Work in a one-on-one situation and learn to execute the basic passes to start a play to the corner man specifically. From a basketball position, make your fake with the ball and extend out to throw a hook pass by the opponent's ear in a quick-flip maneuver. You can change this drill by faking the flip pass high and coming around with a quick bounce pass to a teammate. It is important that you set up quick movement of the ball by faking to create an opening close to the defender between his ear and shoulder or close to his lower body for the bounce past.

Passing the Ball Against Wall

- Select a point on a wall and stand approximately three feet from it. In this maneuver, you pass the ball rapidly against the wall to receive it and pass it again immediately to the wall. This develops good quick hands and rhythm for eye-hand co-ordination.

Dribble Drill—Crossover Dribble

- On a full-length court with the basketball below waist level, take off in a zigzag manner. While dribbling to the right, cross over with a short sharp bounce in front of the body to pick up the dribble with the opposite hand in a continuous motion. Repeat this back and forth across the body for the full length of the court. It is important that you work quickly and control the ball accurately as you move down the court at full speed. It is very important to work at dribbling the ball by keeping the head and eyes up so as to build your confidence and co-ordination in dribbling without looking at the ball.

Dribble Control

- In a small six- or eight-foot area (possibly in a center jump area) have a teammate guard you closely and try to take the ball away. Keep dribbling by spinning and protecting the ball with your back and your body toward your defender. Work hard to keep the ball low and protect it by turning at every attempt the opponent makes to steal or deflect the ball.

Rope Skipping

- Spend time with the rope to develop good rhythm and body co-ordination while using rope-skipping techniques.

Change of Direction-Zigzag Drill

- In basketball it is very important for guards especially to change direction quickly while running. Start by running in a zigzag manner, then change direction sharply by pushing off the outside foot every four or five steps. Do this for the full length of the court and back. Repeat this maneuver several times each day.

Short Spring Running

- To help develop bursts of speed which are so necessary for all basketball players, start running either on a basketball court or a smooth grassy area. Jog in a straight line with periodic ten-yard bursts of speed (sprints). Then jog a short distance. Repeat this several times each day.

One-on-One Defense

- Half-court one-on-one games are excellent competition and provide good work. They should be utilized as much as possible, putting to use the various maneuvers already described.

- A full-court one-on-one game is a tremendous conditioner. Obviously, this game will be of shorter duration than half-court one-on-one games, but much good can be derived out of working hard in a full-court situation, particularly on defensive work versus ball handling skills.

glossary of basketball terms

ASSIST: A pass to a teammate who scores directly or doesn't dribble more than twice before scoring.

BACKDOOR: An offensive maneuver in which a player cuts behind the defensive man and to the basket.

BALL CONTROL: Offensive strategy which prolongs possession of the ball by not shooting until the best possible situation develops. Also referred to as DELIBERATE OFFENSE, DISCIPLINED OFFENSE, STALL BALL, LETTING THE AIR OUT OF THE BALL.

BALL HANDLER: Player who usually brings the ball from his team's backcourt to the front court and initiates the attack. Also referred to as the PLAYMAKER.

BALL HAWK: Player who specializes in recovering loose balls.

BASE LINE: The end boundary line.

BASKET: An 18-inch ring which has a net attached to it. The object of the game is to put the ball through the basket. A team's "own" basket is the one into which team players try to throw the ball. The visiting team has the choice of baskets for the first half and the teams exchange baskets for the second half.

BENCH WARMER: A substitute.

BLOCKING: Personal contact which impedes the progress of an opponent who does not have the ball.

BOARDS: The backboards.

BONUS FREE THROW: A second free throw awarded to a shooter who is successful on his first attempt. This bonus is in effect for each common foul (except a player control foul) committed by a player 'whose team has committed six or more personal fouls in a half (or four or more in a half of a game played in quarters).

CHARITY STRIPE: The free-throw line, thus, the term CHARITY SHOT.

CONTROL: A player is in control when he is holding or dribbling a live ball. Team control exists when a live ball is being passed between members of a team.

CONVERSION: A successful free throw.

CRIPPLE: An easy, unopposed shot at the basket. Also called a CRIB, CRIP SHOT or SNOWBIRD.

DISQUALIFIED PLAYER: A player who is removed from further participation in a game because he has committed his fifth personal foul, or for some other reason such as a flagrant foul.

DOUBLE DRIBBLE: A violation which occurs when a player continues dribbling after grasping the ball with both hands.

DUNKING: Reaching above the rim to put the ball through the basket. Also called a STUFF SHOT. Now a violation in NCAA and high school basketball.

FAST BREAK: Offensive strategy in which a team attempts to bring the ball into scoring position before the defense can set up. Also referred to as RUN AND GUN, RUN AND SHOOT or FIREHOUSE BASKETBALL.

FOUL: A rules infraction for which the penalty is one or more free throws (except in the case of a double foul or a player control foul). Fouls consist of the following types:

> *(a) Common Foul:* A personal foul that is neither flagrant nor intentional nor committed against a player trying for field goal nor part of a double or multiple foul.
>
> *(b) Double Foul:* Opponents commit simultaneous personal fouls against each other.
>
> *(c) Flagrant Foul:* A violent or savage unsportsmanlike act or a non-contact vulgar or abusive display; not necessarily intentional.
>
> *(d) Intentional Foul:* One which the official judges to be designed or premeditated; not based on severity of the act.
>
> *(e) Multiple Foul:* Two or more teammates commit simultaneous personal fouls against the same opponent (a "gang-up").
>
> *(f) Personal Foul:* Involves contact with an opponent while the ball is alive or after the ball is in possession for a throw-in.
>
> *(g) Player Control Foul:* A common foul committed by a player while he or a teammate is in control of the ball.
>
> *(h) Technical Foul:* Usually a non-contact foul by either a player or a non-player; occasionally a contact foul when the ball is dead.
>
> *(i) Unsportsmanlike Foul:* Unfair, unethical or dishonorable conduct.

FREE THROW: Opportunity given to a player to score one point by an unimpeded shot from behind the free-throw line.

FRONT COURT, BACKCOURT: A team's front court is in the area of the court between the mid-court line and its basket. A team's backcourt is the rest of the court including the opponent's basket.

FULL COURT PRESS: Defense strategy in which a team guards the opposition closely in the backcourt as well as the front court. This device can employ both zone and man-to-man principles.

FUMBLE: Accidental loss of control of the ball by dropping it or permitting it to slip out of one's hands.

GIVE AND GO: Offensive strategy in which a player passes to a teammate and then cuts for the basket expecting a return pass.

GOAL TENDING: Touching the ball or the basket while the ball is on, above or within the opponent's basket.

HELD BALL: Occurs when two opponents grasp the ball so firmly that control cannot be maintained without undue roughness; a closely-guarded player (defensive player is no more than six feet away) holds the ball in his front court for five seconds; a team in its front court holds the ball for five seconds in an area enclosed by screening teammates or a closely-guarded player dribbles or combines holding the ball and dribbling for five seconds within a few feet of a front court boundary intersection or in his mid-court area.

HIGH POST: An offensive pivotman who stations himself in or near the outer half of the free-throw circle.

HITCHHIKER: The member of a three-man officiating team who remains fluid near the mid-court line.

HOLDING: Personal contact with an opponent which interferes with his freedom of movement.

HOOP: The basket. Also called the CAGE or the BUCKET.

JUMP BALL: A method of putting the ball in play by tossing it up between two opponents in one of the three circles.

KEY: The free-throw lane and circle. Also called KEYHOLE.

KICKING THE BALL: A violation when done as a positive act. Accidental contact is not a violation.

LOW POST: An offensive maneuver in which the center stations himself just outside the free-throw lane close to the basket.

MAN-TO-MAN DEFENSE: A defensive system in which each player guards an assigned individual.

OVERTIME: One or more extra periods used to break a tie score.

PASS: Movement of the ball from one player to another, usually by throwing, bouncing or rolling along the floor.

PIVOT: Movement in which a player while holding the ball steps any number of times with the same foot, while the other foot (pivot foot) holds its point of contact with the floor.

ROLL: A movement by a screener after his teammate begins a drive off the screen. This is most effective if the defenders are forced to switch and can result in a basket for the man rolling.

SCREEN: A legal method of blocking a defender without causing contact. Screens can be set for moving players as well as stationary players and the player for whom the screen is set may or may not have the ball.

THROW-IN: A method of putting the ball in play from out of bounds.

TIME LINE: The division line across mid-court, so called because the offensive team must advance the ball across it to the front court within ten seconds after gaining possession.

TURNOVER: Any loss of possession without a shot being taken.

TWO (OR THREE) ON ONE: Two (or three) players converging on the basket with only one defensive player to attempt to stop them.

ZONE DEFENSE: A defensive system in which players cover assigned court areas, rather than specific individuals.

Key to Diagrams

① — Offensive player with identifying number

①. — Offensive player with ball

X1 — Defensive player with identifying number

- - - - - -> — Direction of a pass

————> — Direction of movement or a cut by a player

X X X X — Dribbling basketball

①↝ — Cut, jab step, fake with change of direction

———(— Screen or block

notes

notes

notes